Rhyme and Reason

Rhyme and Reason

Collection of Poems for Children

A N A N Y A S. G U H A

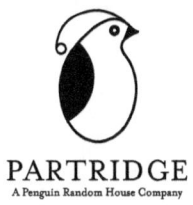

PARTRIDGE
A Penguin Random House Company

To order additional copies of this book, contact
Partridge India
000 800 10062 62
orders.india@partridgepublishing.com

www.partridgepublishing.com/india

Contents

All these poems have been published in the children website: www.bolokids.com earlier, due acknowledgement is made to the editors of this website with gratitude. I am also grateful to my friend Albert Jala for helping me with the checking and editing of the manuscript.

For my daughter Anindita

A Fair Song!

There is a trade fair in my city
to visit it, is a ditty
pots and pans
cups and glasses
but I won't miss classes!
I will visit it in the evening
and walk the stalls
to see if I can buy an overall
or some necklaces
to go to places
all decked up
in my best attire
the trade fair is full of edibles
which makes me gullible
but visit it I must
to be a little bit happy
buying, not crying.
Just!

There is a trade fair in my city
come all of you
sane and witty
buy those tables and chairs
and earthen wares
or some machines
grinders
which are blinders

come all of you
visit
I have already been there once
and, will revisit

Munching chops
cutlets and biryani
spending some money
tastes like honey!

A Fall

I had a fall
bumpity bump
not Humpty Dumpty like
but a fall!
a lot of noise, the bones rattled
the fall was great I was small
a lot of noise, bones creaked
so did hospital doors!

Next time, you have a fall
make sure its not in the Mall!

A Home

A home is a place
see each other face to face
morning, evening, night
the home has a might!
which can never be broken
even when separate
we are not disparate
but individuals who love
flying like the dove.
Father, mother brother, sister
a home binds
is never unkind
sorrows, joys we share
I always want to get there!

A Town I Call Home

There is a town
I call home.
Here buildings rise
and planes fly.
The skyscrapers dusty.
The malls feisty.
Here children and
friends run around.
Merry go round.
The weather is shifty.
Rain, heat, dusty.
And my eyes
become misty.
For my home.
For my town,
called home.

Air Rides!

Air rides are bumpy
clouds are lumpy
looks like little bits of flesh
all in a mesh.
The insides are cool
like sitting in a swimming pool
food being served
I am in my best verve.
Walking up and down is fun
with the nearby sun
but when the weather gets stormy
we are all in a worry.

Praying then is a solution.
That is my resolution.

But once out of the aircraft
we feel we are on a raft!

Air travel is cool and the world around is vast.
We fly with a mast!
It is also fast
So flying is a must.

Book Fair

A book fair
what a fare!
and here I am
browsing
instead of
lousing.

Stalls are many
books are many
I want to pick up any
but the choice is
so large
I can't simply barge

There are stalls which
sell food
looks pretty good

And there is munching
together with book launching
some people on the wings
of poesy.
Come don't be so nosey!
Choose the books
scan the nooks
to choose
you have nothing to lose!

Books to Read

It's a dull day
No play,
Skies are gloomy,
Feel a little weary.
No play,
But books are there
To read.
So that thoughts are in need...
No play
Sunless gloomy day.

But so many books to read.
Friends indeed!

Darkness is a Country

Darkness is a country
and I remain there at night.
Night grows darkness grows.
Am I afraid of darkness?
No, no
But afraid I am of evil in darkness
Oh hark, hark hark
Darkness is round the corner of streets and roads.
See the beggar here
See the beggar there
There is darkness there
Darkness is a see saw battle
Which we know and prattle
A battle with light
and then good night!
Darkness is a country
I remain there only at night
and there it is bright
Darkness is light.

Devil & Evil

There was a Devil
they told me it was Evil
Him or Her?
I asked.
That does not matter
The devil is evil
him or her I asked again
they said do not complain
know, just know that
good will come out
again and again!

I Am...

I am me part tree part branch
I grow like a flower
But in front of enemies cower
I am a dreamer
whose dreams become bigger
Going into huge shapes and sizes
in many many guises
I have ambition to get a good job
handling like the door's knob
I have wishes for my parents,
brothers and sisters
wishes that may not be swept,
but preserved and kept
I am me give all
Good things in life to Me.

If I Were...

If I were just that wee bit old
I would go for a grand search
of gold
The kind of gold that would
give me health
wealth and cavalier times
and I would play the mimes
rhyming with chimes
The kind of gold
which would never make me
old
only a king's palace
without any malice
No power
only the hour
of importunate wealth
sturdy health
And, if I were a wee bit young
I would still go in for that gold
so that I never never grow old!

Internet

Internet is a mad, mad world.
World of dashes and pluses words and mashes,
pictures and gashes.
I love it.
Internet is a flashy world
actors and actresses
hair and tresses long
and short short and long.
I go along.
Internet celebrates
whatever it creates
I run down it up it,
discover faces and laces,
mazes and hazes.
I turn around to see
friends and foes all there.
Where?
In the internet,
a wide web caught in it like cobweb.
I hate it,
go back to it to see stories and histories
cultures and vultures.
Love it.

Internet Friends

On the web there are friends
All over, left over
But they keep on coming back
Writing, chatting, whispering
Time space distance
Matter little
Why should I be little?
This world which now is in a box
Honestly this not hoax
I write on the screen
Where have you been?
Will you not be my friend
For another day?
So that I have my way?
Books to read as well
Pages unfurl the computer
is a box containing history
That's its story, no not idiot (box!)
but forget it, I have it!

Me

I am what I am
who am I?
boy, girl going to school?
athelete which may be a boon?
to the school, country or nation?
so that everyone will mention?
actor, artist or poet
which the world will get to know
and people kow tow?
Forget it
I am what I am school, studies and homework
Lots of paper work, so that in future I am
an officer, who will be a leader.

Is that All?
or is there something else I may be?
A scholar, researcher, and talker
who is the final bidder?

The final bid, when I open the lid
and see casket of surprises
Then I will know what I be
yes Be, come to Me!

Memory

The wind
is it winter?
which will be a winner?
with the sun looking down?
and a shrill wind coming down
like thunder, tearing us asunder!

I will run away from the cold
be bold, for we are not too old

Let us exonerate winter
it is a season after
the bellowing rain and sun

Let us feel its our own.

And winter will be a memory
like blue or raspberry!

Mornings

I get up to face another day
come what may
in the sunshine making hay?
but those books will not let
me off the hook
and homework
is the teacher's handiwork
while outside I learn to play come what may.

Every morning is an opening
of a new day, vistas of origin
not to my chagrin
morning is a splendour
of the day's grandeur
in morning I see the openings
of new horizons, vision
of days to come, years to foresee
till the path winds a little only
a little, nothing like a battle.
Morning is the light of day.

Come what may!

Now

Now, the school is Real
Now the school is Fun
Now the School is like
A Gun! Believe me, always
the teacher is shooting questions!
Now the school is lazy
in days which are hazy!
Now the school is full of din
makes me feel rather thin
Now the school is a garden
especially if there is no warden!

But Now, Now and Now
The School is a Big Big How!

October

October
is a pleasant month
things are cooler
the sun is more tepid
and the rains little more vapid.

October is celebration
Dusserah and festivals
Diwali is round the corner
when crackers and lights
be a burner.

Moreover school will end
for Christmas and New Year
and I will gear
for examinations
which will be a test of my worries
but I am not sorry
for after a big test
I will rest and sleep away dreaming
of the New Year surreptitiously coming!

ANANYA S. GUHA

Old Boys' School Meet

I went to my school's
old boys meet.
We are old
became young then.
Remembered the school
why and when.
Made fun in the midst
of laughter and banter.
Made fun of each other.
There was so much to share together.
Amidst laughter and banter.
Played the sports day
relived it like today.
The sack race.
The walking race.
We raced slow paced.
We are old you see
in an old boys meet
where we got together our feet
and played the game of being young.
Wow, that sure was fun!

Poetry (On Reading It)

I read it with
A glow.
There is a flow.
Words, words, words.
There, rhyme.
And a chime.
Rhythm.
A motion.
I sit in trance.
Want to dance.
To music of words.
Striking chords.
Oh, how I enjoy
This joy
(Of words).
Read it loud.
Shout it loud
Do a jig?
Wearing a wig.
A book.
Don't let it off
The hook!

Prayer

Lord you are powerful
Your creations are wonderful
But you don't like blood lust
Which to many is a must.
The wind is a gust like your many many ways
We are beholden to you for all glory
And in creation we see a wonder
Not destruction, which is tearing us asunder.

Questions And Answers!

If there is an Yes,
is there a No?
What do I know
from yes or no?

That the answers
to questions, maybe
Yes or No, better still
The answer to a question
may be a question.

Then will there be a Yes
or No?
Only know
that questions are answers
Yes or No!

Rhymes and Poems

There are a dozen
rhymes I read.
They chime.
like the clock
which strikes
like a mike.
I read and read
the music flows.
And I am aglow.
Rhymes are poems.
I am smitten,
bitten.
With Rhymes and
Poems.

School Anthem

Do you have one?
We have one
A song, played
to beats and gong
a song of wonder
clap clap clap
school is not a trap
We have here everybody
the good, the bad and the ugly!
Some of us do wonders
if you just look a bit yonder
and many past pupils
have gone streets ahead
in India and abroad
making us All feel proud
The school anthem is a must
to sing and to make the outburst
that ours is a school
with no fool but the wise, where
teachers are nice!

School Has Begun!

Winter is getting over
and I will take cover
under books and studies
the only remedies
for a new year
with friends
to match with trends
books and reading
these will be my headings
occasionally the tv
to update my cv
then the computer
so as not to hinder
learning online
in my bye lane
of the house
where I louse
but what fun
school has begun!

Sports Day...

I love sports day (in school)
Running, shouting
winning or losing,
does that matter
only chatter
of friends, birds and bees
and that of Nature!
Sometimes of course
the teachers matter,
their shouting and scolding.
'Fall in line, fall in line'.
I never fall in line,
my steps go awry,
my body weary
but amidst laughter,
there is something greater
than winning or losing!
So, come Sports Day
my mind is at bay
Come sunshine, rain or thunder
Sports Day is a wonder.

Stories

I love to tell a story
which is ancient,
of the past and hoary.
A story which is not gory.
Not a drop of blood in it
nor a tear
willingly lend to my ear
but violence and scavengers
I'm not interested in such avengers!
A story quiet
but which has a might
with sunshine and laughter
with all the looking after!
I love to listen to a story
a story not at all gory!

Swimming in The Sea

I love to swim
That is a whim
It is a fancy
That drives me crazy
The sea is vast
But go to it I must
The sea is crazy
Sometimes I do feel lazy
But swim I must
That is just
A dream
And when I take the plunge
My fears I must expunge
Even if it is not the sea
Even if it is a stream
The swimming I must dream.

Tea

My cup of tea greets the hills
brewing cup of green green tea
that's me in the morning
black in the evening
after play,
another day.

My cup of tea is brimful
isn't it wonderful
tasty, nice slippery
at play and study
it is a cup of tea
which is my duty!

The House

The house is so tall.
I am small.
The house is big.
And I wear a wig!

There are trees around the house.
I surround.
There are stories about the house.
Stories of ghosts, and what not.

I feel like a mouse.
I am terrified, petrified.
But I love the house.
Even if I am a louse.

Greenery surrounds it.
An old man lives in it.
Cantankerous and noisy.
He seems to be a busy body.

But I really love the house.
Even though I am a louse!
(and a mouse)

The Rain and Wind...

Just a little
bigger than me.
He; but 'little'
all the same,
plays with me,
flies the kite,
sometimes of food
and fruits a bite.

Kicks the ball
has a fall
how naughty is
he and me!

My next door neighbour.
He does me a favour
by giving company
in the rain and wind.
Peace of mind...

The Sun

Winter is my rose garden
the sun tepid, sometimes vapid
yet a burner, what a winner.
The sun in winter
is a forerunner
of summer
but summer is hazy
winter is lazy
the sun meanders
wanders, oranges
give company
I am with many
in happy company
the sun in winter
is a friend, not a fiend
as in summer.

The Sun

The sun now goes mellow.
Yellow.
The sun is a friend,
but sometimes can be a fiend!
When it shines furiously
I argue heatedly!
Go back sun
don't come
your fury erupts
and my mind, it disrupts.
Your yellow
should mellow,
then only do I like
you sun, my friend
in need, but when you
totally vanish the rains I heed!

This Summer...

Summer is appearing
wistfully slowly
as I wait for rains fearfully
Summer is clambering up slopes
and plains
we await patiently the rains
Yet summer makes me wistful
and sometimes forgetful
of what winter is, was
and has.

This summer I will pick up the
rain drops amidst humidity
and play my jaunty jallopy

This summer I will remember
the meandering river
the giver of misfortune
yet a lover.

Tree

The tree with
drooping head
stands outside
like sentinel on guard
What ails it?
In the day its
face lights up
In the night
shadows fall across
looks sad
head and spirits down
Happy happy
it is in the day
when everything
goes our way
At night somnolent
the tree shivers
when the wind quivers
giving me jitters.
In the morning I greet
it with smile
At night I say:
"Good bye!"

Trees

I love them
green o green
skies above.
I love
Trees.

Trees nestle by roads,
gardens, lawns
so many hues;
so many blues,
sometimes they look sad
heads falling.

They are like me
sad, happy,
happy, sad...
their wings are many!

I'll fly on them
soar like a kite,
at play.
I'll fly, fly
(on them)
like a bird on wings.

Trees

The trees touch the sky
and me.
Trees are not animals
but human like me.
So don't cut them into pieces
for that is murder
what a blunder!
Trees suffer death
when cut into pieces
that is murder
what happens then I wonder.

Trees support earth, sky and me.
And, then I love the atmosphere
in a biosphere.
Don't cut
don't murder.
Trees are human like you and me.
Don't you see?

What Do I have?

What do I have?
A house
A mouse
Pet
you bet.

What do I have?
A family
That's my duty

Books, don't let
them off the hook.

Best friends they are
my books
they are not crooks!

What do I have?
a little purse
which does nurse
my jingling coins

What do I have?
A school
which I drool
lovely playgrounds
a white mansion
My mission!

What is A Poem?

What is a poem?
Is it rhyme or time rhythm
or beat making you feel upbeat?
Is it a song or dance?
To which we prance?
Is it story not so gory?
Is it the wind?
Which scatters the mind?
Is it a meandering river
Forget me never?
What is a poem?
Is it jingle In a jungle?
Is it a book?
Letting me off the hook?
Oh never will I forget a poem,
which I love Ever!

What Wishes?

Wishes come to me like rain or storm
then I feel like a worm coiled in thoughts.
I wonder what begets such thoughts.
But wishes can be horses
on which I can ride and bide Time.
For wishes must grow for me
to know what life has in store!
In wishes I dream
make dreams come true
is also my wish
which I know can last to a finish!
Oh wishes, come like a river
like rain and storm
so that I dream,
dream of aspirations
for a life of rejuvenation.

Winter

Winter is near
It is here;
Summer birds have migrated
(I feel a little devastated!)
Mild flutter,
Stutter
Stammer,
Then to play in green fields
With a hammer!
In sky's whisper: 'winter is here
I'm near'.
And, you winter
Are so dear.

Winter

It's winter now
The sun is bright
And I am light
Lighter than the wind
Than the sky
which blows so high
I feel good
In a better better mood
Fields to run around
Like a merry go round
Exams will be over
And friends will be left over
Many to play with
Talk with
Fight with
Oranges will glow
And I will sleep in afternoon
With winter's sun playing the goon
Nights will be cold
The days, old
Oh winter come every day
And take me away!

Wishes

Wishes come to me like rain or storm
then I feel like a worm coiled in thoughts.
I wonder what begets such thoughts.
But wishes can be horses
on which I can ride and bide Time.
For wishes must grow for me
to know what life has in store!
In wishes I dream
make dreams come true
is also my wish
which I know can last to a finish!
Oh wishes, come like a river
like rain and storm
so that I dream,
dream of aspirations
for a life of rejuvenation.

World Of Imagination!

I love to fly like a kite
having a bite
of clouds and skies
these are not lies
these are fantasies
of little mercies
flying is not lying
it is imagining
soaring and laughing
sometimes, out of fear
crying.

I love to fly like a bird
soaring
wavering
trembling
but not grumbling!

I love to fly into a world
away from this
which I will not miss
for that world
is in my mind, my imagination
and that will go on for a generation.

Writing...

Love to write
right or wrong?
Can you tell me a story
that long?
So that equipped with pen
I will write
with all my might
write of bamboos and rivers
kind people and givers
People of all hues
to get rid of my blues
My friends and all
who give me a wonderful call
making me feel Tall, Tall
as I stand in the school hall.

Write of sunshine and rain
which are nature in the main
write of animals
and gobbles
mammals and camels.

To write is to see a hood
of human good.

Ananya S Guha
Shillong, India

www.ingramcontent.com/pod-product-compliance
Lightning Source LLC
Chambersburg PA
CBHW051248170526
45165CB00004B/1622